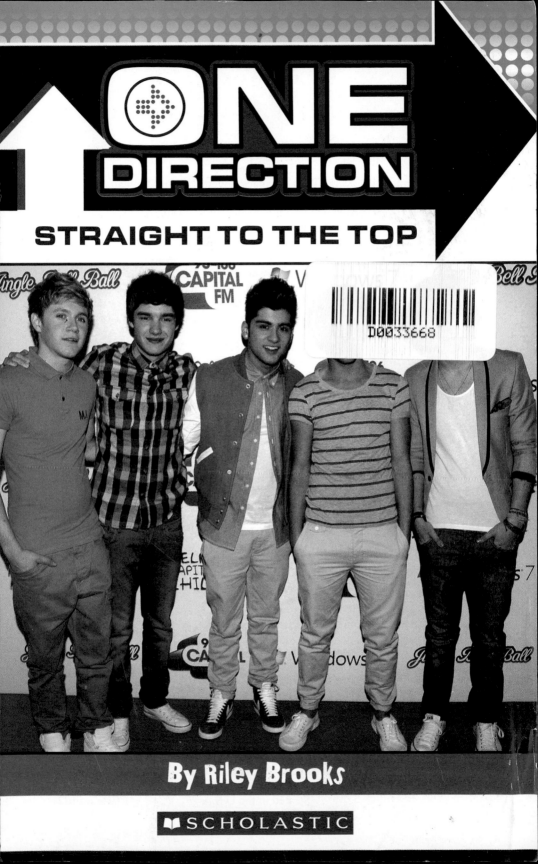

ONE DIRECTION

STRAIGHT TO THE TOP

D0033668

By Riley Brooks

SCHOLASTIC

Photo credits:
Front cover: © Ian West/AP; back cover: © John Marshall /AP
p. 1: © Rex Features/Associated Press; p. 4: © Ian West/Associated Press;
p. 5: © Ian West/Associated Press; p. 6: © Anthony Devlin/Associated Press;
p. 8: © Charles Sykes/Associated Press; p. 9: © Owen Sweeney/Rex Features/Associated
Press; p. 10: © Anthony Devlin/Associated Press; p. 12: © Charles Sykes/Associated
Press; p. 13: © Ian West/Associated Press; p. 14: © Stewart Cook/Rex Features/
Associated Press; p. 16: © Owen Sweeney/Rex Features/Associated Press;
p. 17: © Charles Sykes/Associated Press; p. 18: © Charles Sykes/Associated Press;
p. 20: © Charles Sykes/Associated Press; p. 21: © Charles Sykes/Associated Press;
p. 22: © Charles Sykes/Associated Press; p. 24: © Arthur Mola/Associated Press;
p. 25: © Charles Sykes/Associated Press; p. 26: © Dominic Lipinski/Associated Press;
p. 29: © Ian West/Associated Press; p. 30: © Yui Mok/Associated Press;
p. 31: © David Rowland/Rex Features/Associated Press; p. 32: © AGF s.r.l./Rex
Features/Associated Press; p. 34: © Frank Micelotta/Associated Press; p. 35: © John
Marshall/Associated Press; p. 36: © Charles Sykes/Associated Press; p. 38: © David
Rowland/Rex Features/Associated Press; p. 39: © Nikki To/Rex Features/Associated
Press; p. 40: © Yui Mok/Associated Press; p. 42: © Charles Sykes/Associated Press;
p. 43: © Ian West/Associated Press; p. 44: © Frank Micelotta/Associated Press;
p. 46: © Chris Pizzello/Associated Press; p. 47: © David Rowland/Rex Features/
Associated Press; p. 48: © IBL/Rex Features/Associated Press
Sticker sheet: pink hearts: © MarketOlya/Shutterstock; stars: © beboy/Shutterstock;
guitars: © Monkik/Shutterstock; peace sign: © vectomart/Shutterstock;
microphone: © DVARG/Shutterstock; shooting yellow star: © Oculo/Shutterstock;
music notes: © zphoto/Shutterstock.

ISBN 978-0-545-49988-0

SCHOLASTIC and associated logos are trademarks and/or registered
trademarks of Scholastic Inc.

12 11 10 9 8 7 6 5 4 3 2 1   12 13 14 15 16/0

Printed in the U.S.A   132
First printing, September 2012

Table of Contents

Introduction

The first time One Direction appeared together on stage, they were five very nervous boys who barely knew each other. They were performing on *The X Factor* and were worried they were going to be sent home. But these days the guys of 1D—Niall, Zayn, Liam, Harry, and Louis—are as close as brothers!

Now One Direction is taking the music world by storm with a number one album, sold-out concerts, and plenty of adoring fans. Despite their newfound fame, boys will be boys, and the boys of One Direction are every bit as fun and down-to-earth as their fans imagine them to be!

CHAPTER 1

Niall Horan

Adorable blond Niall James Horan was born on September 13, 1993, in Ireland. His parents, Maura and Bobby, split up when Niall was five, but they have both always been very supportive of his dreams.

Niall's dad and aunt knew they had a star on their hands when one day they heard him singing in the car and thought the radio was on! "Exactly the same thing happened to Michael Bublé with his dad," Niall explained to digitalspy.com. "He's my absolute hero so I like the fact we have a similar story." Niall's family was very proud of his talent. They got him a guitar for Christmas and he has been playing ever since.

Niall's talent set him apart from the other students at his school, Coláiste Mhuire. In fact, Niall sang in a few local concerts while he was in school. All of those performances helped Niall prepare for his *X Factor* audition, but he was still pretty nervous on the big day! He stood in line with over 10,000 other hopefuls to sing for just a few minutes. Luckily, Niall made a big impression and was invited to continue with the competition.

Full Name: Niall James Horan

Nickname: Kyle

Birthday: September 13, 1993

Siblings: older brother, Greg

Hometown: Mullingar, Ireland

Favorite Movie: *Grease*

Favorite Bands: The Script, Ed Sheeran, Bon Jovi

Dislikes: mayonnaise

Twitter Handle: @NiallOfficial

Star Stats

CHAPTER 2

Zayn Malik

Zain Javadd Malik, better known as Zayn, was born on January 12, 1993. Zayn gets his charm from his British Pakistani father, Yaser, and his energy from his British mother, Tricia. "I was a bit of a handful when I was a kid because I was quite hyperactive . . ." Zayn told thesun.co.uk. Zayn has always been proof that good things come in small packages—Zayn was one of the shortest kids in his classes, but his big personality more than made up for it!

Along with his three younger sisters, Doniya, Waliyha, and Safaa, Zayn grew up in East Bowling, England. Things weren't always easy for Zayn. He and his sisters were often bullied because of their mixed heritage, and they had to change schools several times.

Things got better for Zayn when he began school at Tong High School, where he joined the theatre program. As soon as Zayn got up on stage, he was completely comfortable in the spotlight. Steve Gates, a teacher at Tong High, told thetelegraphandargus.co.uk, "Zayn is a model student who excelled in all the performing arts subjects . . . He was always a star performer in all the school productions." So, it was really no surprise to anyone when Zayn decided to audition for *The X Factor*—his friends and family already knew he was a star!

CHAPTER 3

Liam Payne

Liam James Payne gave his parents, Karen and Geoff, quite a scare when he was born on August 29, 1993, in Wolverhampton, England. Little Liam had health problems from the moment he took his first breath. He told sugarscape.com, "They discovered that one of my kidneys wasn't working properly and it had scarred . . . I have to be careful not to drink too much, even water, and I have to keep myself as healthy as possible." Luckily, Liam's parents and older sisters, Ruth and Nicola, always took great care of him!

In high school, Liam was one of the stars on the cross-country team. He also took boxing lessons.

When Liam wasn't playing sports, he focused on music. Liam studied music technology at the City of Wolverhampton College. He had considered a job behind the scenes in the music business, but Liam always secretly dreamed of being a singer. He had actually auditioned for *The X Factor* back in 2008, but didn't make it very far. Simon Cowell encouraged him to come back in two years—and it's a good thing he did, since the second time around landed Liam in One Direction!

Star Stats

Full Name: Liam James Payne

Nickname: Ian

Birthday: August 29, 1993

Siblings: older sisters, Ruth and Nicola

Hometown: Wolverhampton, England

Favorite Movie: all three Toy Story films

Favorite Bands: Bing Crosby, Two Door Cinema Club, John Mayer

Known As: the "Dad" of 1D

Twitter Handle: @Real_Liam_Payne

CHAPTER 4

Harry Styles

Harry Edward Styles was born on February 1, 1994, in Evesham, England. His parents, Anne and Des, knew early on that they had a star on their hands—Harry always loved singing, especially Elvis Presley's songs. Harry's parents got a divorce when he was seven, but he and his older sister, Gemma, always got to spend plenty of time with both parents growing up.

As Harry got older, his love of music really took center stage. While attending Holmes Chapel Comprehensive School, Harry became the lead singer for the band White Eskimo with friends Haydn Morris, Nick Clough, and Will Sweeny. Harry's bubbly personality made him the perfect front man for the band. They performed at school events, Battle of the Bands, and even at a wedding! Then, Harry decided to audition for *The X Factor*. He initially entered as a solo performer. He sang "Isn't She Lovely" by Stevie Wonder and really had fun with it. But Harry had to leave his bandmates behind when he made it through the first auditions. Luckily, Harry's White Eskimo friends have been really supportive and are big One Direction fans.

Star Stats

Full Name: Harry Edward Styles

Nickname: Barry

Birthday: February 1, 1994

Siblings: older sister, Gemma

Hometown: Holmes Chapel, England

Favorite Movie: *Love Actually*

Favorite Bands: The Beatles, Foster the People, Coldplay, Kings of Leon

Best Friend: Louis Tomlinson

Twitter Handle: @Harry_Styles

CHAPTER 5

Louis Tomlinson

Johanna and Mark Tomlinson got a fantastic early Christmas present when Louis William Tomlinson was born on December 24, 1991, in Doncaster, England. Soon the Tomlinson family grew to include younger sisters Charlotte, Félicité, and twins Daisy and Phoebe. When their parents split up in 2002, Louis really stepped up to take the best care of his sisters possible.

It was clear that the Tomlinson kids all had talent at a very young age. Daisy and Phoebe started acting as babies on the popular British TV show *Fat Friends*. Louis was an extra on the same show, had a role in the made-for-TV movie *If I Had You*, and appeared on *Waterloo Road*, an award-winning British television series. Louis loved being in front of the camera, but music was always his biggest passion.

Louis attended Hall Cross School for high school, where he starred in the school's musicals and plays. Since Louis had always loved being in the spotlight, it was no surprise to any of his classmates that he auditioned for *The X Factor* and joined One Direction. Everyone was really proud of Louis for achieving his dreams and they are all cheering him on from back home.

Star Stats

Full Name: Louis William Tomlinson

Nickname: Hughy

Birthday: December 24, 1991

Siblings: younger sisters, Charlotte, Félicité, Daisy, and Phoebe

Hometown: Doncaster, England

Favorite Movie: *Grease*

Favorite Bands: The Fray, Bombay Bicycle Club

Best Friend: Harry Styles

Twitter Handle: @Louis_Tomlinson

CHAPTER 6

X Marks the Spot

*T*he *X Factor* is one of the hottest shows in the United Kingdom. (In fact, it was such a hit, they made a version for the U.S.!) Fans tune in every season to watch hopefuls audition to compete for a recording contract. Contestants can enter in one of four categories—boys, girls, over-twenty-five-year-olds, or groups.

After several rounds of open auditions, select contestants go through a boot camp and mentoring before one final audition. The remaining contestants then compete on live TV each week for viewers' votes. Getting past the first round of auditions is a big deal, but getting to the live finals is a dream come true for any singer—and the boys of One Direction are no exception.

Liam, Harry, Niall, Louis, and Zayn each auditioned in their hometowns for the chance to compete on 2010's seventh season in the boys category. Each of the guys picked songs to show off their unique styles. All five of the guys made it to the boot-camp round, but then they ran into trouble. Zayn had an especially difficult time with the dancing. Unfortunately, none of the guys made it through the boot-camp round.

That would have been the end of the story if the judges hadn't had a brilliant idea. They suggested that Liam, Harry, Niall, Louis, and Zayn form a boy band and continue through the competition as a group. It was an interesting proposal, as Zayn explained to teenvogue.com: "Before we got together as a band we were kind of each other's competition because we're from the same category [on *X Factor*]. But as soon as we got put together we all got on really well. We all went to Harry's place and stayed there together to get to know each other."

The boys only had a short time to get their new act together, and an even shorter time to come up with a name for their group. Harry suggested One Direction since all of the boys had the same goal, and, with that, One Direction was born!

The rest of the competition was tough, but the guys did a great job. They made it all the way to the final round singing songs like "My Life Would Suck Without You," "Kids in America," and "Chasing Cars." Sadly, One Direction didn't win. They finished in third place. Fans were disappointed, but they cheered up when "Forever Young," a single One Direction had recorded in case they won, was leaked on the Internet!

Usually, only the winner of *The X Factor* gets a recording contract, but one of the judges, Simon Cowell (former *American Idol* judge), offered One Direction a contract with his record label, Syco Records. After a four-month *X Factor* tour, One Direction went straight into the recording studio to create their first album.

CHAPTER 7

Up All Night

Recording an album was a totally new experience for One Direction, but it was a challenge they were ready for! "Thankfully, we got lots of say in the album, actually," Liam told irishtimes.com. "We got to choose a lot of the songs and that sort of stuff . . ." The guys even helped write some of the songs they recorded! Zayn told irishtimes.com, "When you write your own music . . . it can be quite hard to express it to people. But we always felt comfortable. And we had each other to show our ideas to."

One Direction's first single, "What Makes You Beautiful," was released on September 11, 2011, in the UK and it immediately shot to number one on the UK Singles Chart. "Gotta Be You," the guys' second single was released on November 13, 2011, and their debut album, *Up All Night*, hit store shelves a week later on November 21, 2011. The album rocketed to number two on the UK charts and quickly reached the top ten in eighteen other countries.

One Direction promoted their album with appearances on TV shows, radio stations, and at award shows. The guys won the 2011 4Music Awards for "Best Group," "Best

Breakthrough," and "Best Video," and beat out Adele to win the 2012 Brit Award for "Best British Single" for "What Makes You Beautiful." The Brit awards are a really high achievement—they're like the Grammy Awards in America. They also went on tour all over the United Kingdom, with most shows selling out within minutes. It was official: One Direction was a pop sensation in the UK.

CHAPTER 8

The New British Invasion

O ne Direction wasn't just content with being the UK's favorite boy band—they wanted to conquer the whole world! One Direction made history on March 13, 2012, when they released *Up All Night* at number one on the American charts. They were the first British group to ever have a number one debut in the U.S. "We simply cannot believe that we are number one in America," Harry told cbsnews.com. "It's beyond a dream come true for us."

Liam, Zayn, Niall, Harry, and Louis spent a lot of time in America promoting their album. They made appearances to meet their U.S. fans and sign autographs, opened for American boy band Big Time Rush on a leg of their sold-out "Better With U" Tour, and made guest appearances on several TV shows including Nickelodeon's *iCarly* and *The Today Show* on March 12, 2012. Over 10,000 fans came out to see them perform that morning on *The Today Show*. "It was incredible," Liam told hitflix.com. "When we came to the front of the stage and saw how many people there were, it was literally my most amazing moment so far." One Direction even performed as the musical guest on the

April 7, 2011, episode of *Saturday Night Live*, the guys' favorite comedy show!

With their singles and album racing up the U.S. charts, One Direction announced a summer U.S. tour, which sold out in record time. The guys also performed "What Makes You Beautiful" at the 2012 *Nickelodeon Kids' Choice Awards*. The performance was definitely one of the favorites of the night. The guys are also in discussions with Nickelodeon to develop a show. How cool would that be?

U.S. fans can't seem to get enough of One Direction, and it's clear that the British invasion won't be stopping anytime soon!

CHAPTER 9

Backstage Pass

The guys of One Direction spend a LOT of time together, so it's a good thing that they get along so well. Since the guys can't take their families and friends on tour with them, they've become like family to each other. Louis and Harry even rented an apartment together in North London!

When they aren't touring or working, the guys try to catch up with their families and friends as much as they can! "[Our moms] all got the same sort of mom thing where they're all really upset when . . . we leave home, but at the same time they know we're going out and enjoying what we do. But they miss us," Liam told teenvogue.com. The boys check in with lots of phone calls and e-mails, but nothing is as good as a visit home! "[O]bviously it's a great experience for us, but also we also make our moms proud. We've found friends in each other, but also our parents are friends," Louis explained to teenvogue.com.

One Direction spends a lot of time on the road these days, but the guys know how to make their work fun. They have a blast goofing off in their hotels, shooting funny videos to post for their fans, playing pranks on one another, listening to music, watching

movies, and ordering room service!

Of course, the guys try to check out cool places in every city they visit. They love to go out to eat and see the sites and take a break from work. So don't be surprised if you see Zayn, Niall, Harry, Liam, or Louis out and about in your town if they have a concert nearby!

CHAPTER 10

Fab Future

One Direction's career is just getting warmed up. With a number one album, chart-topping singles, and tour dates, the guys are very busy. But, luckily for One Direction's fans, Liam, Harry, Zayn, Louis, and Niall aren't slowing down anytime soon!

The group plans to record their next album by the end of 2012. Niall told *The National Post*, "In the summer, we're going to get back and start a new record. We want to bring out a record nearly every year/every year and a half." The guys have already started working on new songs and are meeting with producers. "I think we'd like to do more writing on the next album," Liam told hitflix.com. Writing great new songs and recording music that their fans will love is always going to be the band's number one priority.

As important as their music is, One Direction has lots of other opportunities coming their way, too. They have a development deal in place with Nickelodeon for a TV show and have signed on to partner with some cool brands like Pokémon and Nokia. The guys would love to possibly work on a clothing line, make some movie appearances, and headline

a global tour! "The ultimate goal would be to do a big, worldwide tour. That would be the most amazing thing we could do," Liam told suntimes.com. So keep your eyes peeled for a 1D show near you soon!

One thing is certain, no matter what the future holds, it's looking very bright for the cuties of One Direction!

1D Online

Want more info on One Direction?

Check out their official sites:

Official Website: www.onedirectionmusic.com

Official Twitter: @onedirection

Official Facebook: www.facebook.com/onedirectionmusic